T0383397

COCKTAILS AT LARRY'S

COCKTAILS

AT

LARRY'S

BY
TOM ONIONS

NATIONAL PORTRAIT GALLERY, LONDON
IN COLLABORATION WITH
THE DAISY GREEN COLLECTION

WELCOME TO LARRY'S

Larry's is an award-winning underground speakeasy, located at the heart of London's acclaimed National Portrait Gallery, home to the world's greatest collection of portraits.

Located in former 18th-century coal cellars equidistant between the refined grandeur of Whitehall and Buckingham Palace and the world-famous theatres and clubs of Leicester Square, Covent Garden and Soho, Larry's is a homage to the creative and cultural melting pot that is – and always has been – London.

Our speakeasy and signature cocktail are named after the renowned actor, producer and director Sir Laurence Olivier, who for over half a century headlined the West End's fabled stages, while insisting that everyone call him simply, 'Larry'.

The cocktails in this book toast the many famous faces from the National Portrait Gallery's Collection who are treasured for their contributions to fields including theatre, film, the visual arts, music and fashion; and we celebrate the photographers who captured the iconic images shown here.

We take an in-depth look at the West End throughout time with its multi-generational, ever-evolving cast of characters – from Cecil Beaton socialising with the glamorous 'Bright Young Things' at the Gargoyle Club, to Francis Bacon once again climbing up the steps to his beloved Colony Room.

From the Gin Fizz to the Margarita, we have put our twist on the cocktails you know and love, to delight your tastebuds while you take in the images and the stories of those who inspired them.

This is not a bible of cocktails or a book of history. It seeks to capture the moment at which these drinks were enjoyed – from the original White Lady at Ciro's to the Espresso Martini at Fred's in the naughty noughties – and the amazing people who have brought the West End to life: surviving wars, challenging norms and creating change.

7

THE COCKTAILS

LARRY'S

ABOVE: Laurence Olivier by Yousuf Karsh, 1954

NEXT SPREAD: Laurence Olivier and Vivien Leigh by an unknown photographer, 1937

Laurence Olivier, or 'Larry' as he liked to be known, was widely regarded as one the greatest British actors of the 20th century. He enjoyed his first West End success in Noël Coward's *Private Lives* in 1930, and later came to be recognised as one of the most explosive Shakespearean actors, bringing a new physicality to the stage.

It was through theatre and film that he met Vivien Leigh, and they fell in love when filming *Fire Over England* in 1937, before travelling to Denmark to stage *Hamlet* in the place where it was set, on the ramparts of Kronborg Castle. *Hamlet* was a sensation, sealing Olivier's reputation as one of most dazzling actors of his day, and soon his romance with Leigh would captivate the world.

In 1939 Olivier travelled to America to star in *Wuthering Heights* alongside Merle Oberon, and Leigh followed by boat. It was while in America that she won her first Oscar as Scarlett O'Hara in *Gone with the Wind* (1939), and together Olivier and Leigh became superstars, marrying in 1940.

Olivier continued to direct, earning a knighthood for his services to stage and film in 1947. From 1962 to 1973 he was the Founding Director of London's National Theatre, and some of Britain's most talented actors performed under his direction.

Laurence Olivier and Vivien Leigh famously loved throwing and attending glamorous cocktail parties, where strong spirits were served. We can imagine them sipping many an Old Fashioned.

LARRY'S: OLD FASHIONED

Jura 10 Scotch whisky
GlenDronach 12 Scotch whisky
Homemade cereal syrup
Cherry bitters, to spray
Cherry, to garnish

Rich and sweet, with notes of cherry

The first Old Fashioned is thought to have been created at
the Pendennis Club in Kentucky, before it was popularised
at the Waldorf Astoria Hotel bar in New York City. We have selected
the Old Fashioned to celebrate Laurence Olivier – a tongue-in-cheek
reference to his love of early literature and Shakespeare, but also
because it is one of the most physically demanding cocktails to make
(requiring up to five minutes of continuous stirring) – not quite the
same as Olivier's theatrical strength, but hard hitting nonetheless!

Our twist on the classic Old Fashioned uses Scotch whisky instead of
bourbon. We have blended our Scotch whisky with a rich cereal syrup
and a touch of cherry bitters, to evoke the feel of bourbon.
Our cereal syrup mixes corn, barley, rye and toasted rice, slow-cooked
for 50 minutes at 48 degrees celsius.

THE YEVONDE

ABOVE: Yevonde self-portrait, 1937
NEXT SPREAD: Melita Bell and an unidentified model by Yevonde, 1935

Just as the world of cinema evolved from black
and white to colour, so did Yevonde's photography.

Yevonde, also known as Madame Yevonde, was a London-based
photographer of portraits and still life, working throughout much
of the 20th century. She was a pioneer in photographic techniques,
experimenting with solarisation (which used extreme overexposure
to reverse tones), and was associated with the Vivex colour process
in the 1930s. With this technique, Yevonde would take three
photographs in quick succession, develop them in cyan, magenta
and yellow, and overlay them to stunning effect.

'If we are going to have colour photographs, for heaven's sake
let's have a riot of colour, none of your wishy washy hand-tinted
effects' said Yevonde.

As an innovator committed to colour photography at a time when
it was not considered a serious medium, Yevonde's work is
significant in the history of British portrait photography. Her
best-known body of work is a series of images of women dressed
as goddesses, posed in surreal tableaux, exhibited in 1935. The
National Portrait Gallery holds over 2000 photographic negatives
by Yevonde.

Our original cocktail has been specially developed to celebrate
Yevonde's colour photography technique, which printed layers
of cyan, magenta and yellow upon each other.

THE YEVONDE: GIN FIZZ

Gin, infused with lemon myrtle
Elderflower liqueur
Muyu Vetiver Gris liqueur
Citrus solution
Blood orange and elderflower tonic
Cyan, magenta and yellow jelly dots,
    to garnish

Fruity, bubbly and colourful

Henry C. Ramos invented the Ramos Gin Fizz in 1888 at the Imperial Cabinet Saloon in Louisiana. It was originally called a 'New Orleans Fizz' and is one of Louisiana's most famous cocktails. The cocktail became so popular that during the 1915 Mardi Gras season, Ramos employed 35 bartenders, as each serving took 12 minutes to create.

Our Gin Fizz is a twist on this iconic cocktail, with elegant floral notes of lemon myrtle and elderflower, and a splash of dry vermouth to balance the sweetness. Our cocktail is clarified and, instead of using the usual double cream, our citrus and tonic is added from a siphon, followed by jelly dots in cyan, magenta and yellow, to represent Yevonde's sumptuous Vivex photography process.

Our own homemade coloured jelly dot garnishes have tasting notes of dragonfruit puree, butterfly pea flower tea, and fresh lemon juice.

THE BEATON

ABOVE: Cecil Beaton self-portrait, 1930s
NEXT SPREAD: Queen Elizabeth II by Cecil Beaton, 1968

Cecil Beaton was one of the most celebrated photographers of the 20th century. His acclaimed work can be found throughout Larry's, from the glamorous portrait of Audrey Hepburn at the ground-floor entrance, to the portraits of Marilyn Monroe that hang by the bar. The large camera that he used was designed by Condé Nast to produce extra large negatives that he could then mark up by hand.

His work is synonymous with the glamorous and stylish 'Bright Young Things' of the 1920s, whom he often captured on film. This eccentric, glamorous and creative group combined high society and the avant-garde: artists and writers, socialites and partygoers, who often frequented London's Gargoyle Club.

But Beaton's talents were not just limited to photography. He was also a highly acclaimed interior designer, diarist, painter and fashion designer. In 1964 he won multiple Oscars for his production and costume design for the film *My Fair Lady*, which starred Audrey Hepburn. Hepburn herself described owning a Beaton as 'like owning a beautiful painting'.

Beaton's photographs of the British royal family were central to shaping their public image in the mid-20th century. Queen Elizabeth II was still a young princess when she first sat for Beaton. Over the next three decades he would be invited to photograph her on many significant occasions, including her Coronation Day in 1953. For that reason, our Beaton-inspired Bramble includes a twist incorporating what was said to be the Queen's favourite drink, the Dubonnet and Gin.

THE BEATON: DUBONNET AND GIN BRAMBLE

Dubonnet

Bombay Bramble gin, infused with
    summer berries

Sparkling rosé wine

Homemade raspberry and strawberry jam

Violette bitters, to spray

White chocolate coin, with crystallised violet
    and gold dust, to garnish

Crème de Violette fragrance

Big, bold berry and subtle herbal flavour

Dubonnet was invented in 1846 by a Parisian wine merchant and chemist who combined fortified red wine with a secret blend of herbs and spices. Like tonic water, Dubonnet contains quinine, making it a similarly natural partner for gin, a combination that was reputedly a favourite of Queen Elizabeth II. The Queen is said to have preferred a 2:1 ratio of Dubonnet to gin. We have based our Dubonnet and gin cocktail on the Bramble, with its genteel and quintessentially British blackberry flavour profile, created by Dick Bradsell in Soho during the 1980s.

The cocktail is garnished with a homemade sugared-violet white chocolate coin, representing the Queen's love of chocolate, flowers, and floral tastes. Our gin is infused with raspberry and strawberry, vacuum sealed and cooked sous vide at 48 degrees celsius for 50 minutes. The homemade jam includes raspberry, strawberry and raspberry leaves.

THE MONROE

ABOVE: Marilyn Monroe by Cecil Beaton, 1956
NEXT SPREAD: Marilyn Monroe by Cecil Beaton, 1956

London's West End has hosted many of the world's greatest icons, and in 1957, Laurence Olivier starred in and co-produced *The Prince and the Showgirl* in London, alongside co-star and co-producer Marilyn Monroe. The film itself received mixed reviews, but there was great excitement as Monroe – who was then at the height of her fame – spent time exploring the West End with her playwright husband Arthur Miller.

One of the most iconic figures of the 20th century, Monroe had been discovered while modelling and signed contracts with Twentieth Century Fox and later Columbia Pictures. In her short film career, she appeared in some of the most popular films of all time, including *Gentlemen Prefer Blondes* (1953) and *The Seven Year Itch* (1955), creating and managing a public persona that endures today. Such was the strength of her career that in 1954 Monroe started her own production company, and *The Prince and the Showgirl*, based on a script she had purchased, was her first independent production.

Monroe later won a Golden Globe for Best Actress in *Some Like it Hot* (1959), directed by Billy Wilder, who had also directed Vivien Leigh in *Sunset Boulevard* in 1950 and Audrey Hepburn in *Sabrina* in 1954. *The Misfits* (1961), written by Miller during their time in London, was Monroe's last completed film. Shortly after its release, she received a Golden Globe for World Film Favourite.

Monroe, like her roles, has become timeless. The images of her taken by Cecil Beaton have inspired our beautiful, light Martini with rose petals and lychee.

THE MONROE: LYCHEE AND ROSE PETAL MARTINI

Konik's Tail vodka

Lanique Spirit of Rose liqueur

Briottet lychee liqueur

Apricot liqueur

Cadello 88

Lime juice

Rose petal and frozen yogurt coconut
    tear, to garnish

Delicate, luxurious and floral

The allure and charm that Marilyn Monroe exuded on screen have become synonymous with beauty, and we endeavour to conjur her inimitable glamour with our meticulously crafted Lychee and Rose Petal Martini.

Lanique, a key component of this cocktail, traces its origins back to the 18th century. Made from rose petals, Lanique was favoured by nobility for its luxurious aroma and delicate flavour. The Martini itself has its history in the 19th century; it is believed to have evolved out of the Martinez (a drink of gin, vermouth, maraschino liqueur and bitters) created in the town of Martinez in California. Fruit-based cocktails are very much a product of the later 20th century, with a growing following today, which seems only appropriate for one of the greatest and most enduring global icons.

OPPOSITE: **The Monroe**

THE McBEAN

ABOVE: Angus McBean self-portrait, *c.*1951

NEXT SPREAD: The Beverley Sisters by Angus McBean, 1960

Angus McBean was a contemporary of Cecil Beaton, but while Beaton chose to focus on fashion and film, McBean chose to focus on theatre, beginning his career at 15 as a mask-maker and set designer, and later becoming a celebrated photographer.

McBean's work is distinct for its combination of surrealism, elegance and glamour. His studio was in London's West End at Endell Street near Covent Garden, and between the 1930s and 1960s his photography graced nearly every theatre in England. He worked on major productions of Shakespeare's *Hamlet* and *Macbeth*, developing close relationships with Laurence Olivier and Vivien Leigh.

McBean's big break came through playwright Ivor Novello who asked him to create masks for a play he was producing, starring a young Vivien Leigh, beginning a famed 'romance through the lens' between Leigh and McBean. Famously it was a McBean photograph of Leigh that led to her winning her first iconic role as Scarlett O'Hara in *Gone with the Wind* (1939). McBean photographed Leigh for nearly every performance until her death, 30 years later.

In the 1950s and 60s he photographed many of the greats – from Audrey Hepburn to Shirley Bassey, the Beverley Sisters and The Beatles.

In homage to McBean's beautiful and classical images, we have selected a classic cocktail which has stood the test of time and which was also said to be one of Vivien Leigh's favourites: the Martini.

THE MᶜBEAN: DIRTY MARTINI

Highclere Castle London dry gin and
  Gattertop Botanic No.7 vodka,
  cooked sous vide with lemongrass
  and nocellara olives
Asahara Shuzo nigori umeshu
Dry vermouth
A drop of black olive oil

Smooth, cold and sophisticated

Larry's award-winning Dirty Martini, infused and clarified with green olives and lemongrass to extract the citrusy flavour, is served clear and made 'dirty' with a single drop of black olive oil.

Our use of umeshu plum liqueur offers a modern interpretation on the Dirty Martini, while the vodka and gin base brings a strong botanical flavour profile and depth to the drink.

In fact, a combined 17 botanicals are present within Highclere Castle London dry gin and Gattertop Botanic No.7 vodka. Each spirit is derived from organic ingredients foraged from its respective British estate, adding to the citrusy and salty flavours of the Martini.

THE HEPBURN

ABOVE: Audrey Hepburn by Bassano Ltd, 1950
NEXT SPREAD: Audrey Hepburn by Angus McBean, 1950

In 1950, Audrey Hepburn began her long career in film and theatre, performing as a dancer in a musical revue at Ciro's nightclub on Orange Street, in the building that is now the archive and offices of the National Portrait Gallery.

Hepburn's star was in ascendance: that same year, she was photographed by Angus McBean, whose iconic images lent his signature surreal style to her glamour. She gained her first major film role as a ballerina in *The Secret People* (1952). The French author Colette saw her on set and insisted the young actress be cast in the Broadway version of her novella, *Gigi*. The success of that performance led Hepburn to be chosen to star opposite Hollywood legend, Gregory Peck, in the 1953 film, *Roman Holiday*, for which she won the Academy Award for Best Actress.

Naturally gifted at dance, the young Hepburn had studied ballet in the Netherlands, while also working for the Dutch resistance, during World War II. After the war ended, she came to London to study ballet under the tutelage of Marie Rambert. Her poise and grace were her hallmarks throughout her acting career. The Bassano image of Hepburn as a ballerina opposite was taken to promote *The Secret People*.

33

Our White Lady, inspired by Hepburn, takes the signature cocktail of Ciro's nightclub as its starting point, and adds a fresh, elegant twist.

THE HEPBURN: WHITE LADY

English gin, cold-infused with fresh mint

Cointreau

Green Chartreuse

Clarified lemon mint bitters

Fine Earl Grey tea and lemon foam

Mint leaf, to garnish

Fresh, minty and elegant

The original recipe of the White Lady was created in 1919 by Harry MacElhone, at Ciro's nightclub, where Audrey Hepburn would later begin her career as a dancer. MacElhone created another version of the recipe in 1929 at Harry's New York Bar in Paris, which included hints of mint, and provides the inspiration for our cocktail.

Our White Lady combines mint and gin, which are vacuum-sealed together at -19 degrees celsius for 60 minutes, to extract flavour without drawing the bitterness from the mint leaves. It is served with a refreshing foam, infused with Earl Grey tea and lemon.

HOLLYWOOD HELLRAISERS

ABOVE: Peter O'Toole by Bob Willoughby, 1962
NEXT SPREAD: Elizabeth Taylor by Angus McBean, 1966

Peter O'Toole was the first actor to play Hamlet at the National Theatre under Laurence Olivier and starred with Audrey Hepburn in *How to Steal a Million* (1966). Earlier he had achieved global acclaim for his portrayal of T.E. Lawrence in *Lawrence of Arabia* (1962), which received seven Oscars.

However, outside the screens and stages of the West End, he was creating a very different reputation alongside some of the most talented actors of his generation: Richard Burton, Oliver Reed and Richard Harris. The four could be seen frequently drinking in the pubs and bars of London's West End and have fondly gone down in history as 'hellraisers', with O'Toole once purchasing a pub with Peter Finch when last orders was called, in order to keep the party going.

O'Toole went on to be nominated for eight Oscars, one more than Burton, who, as well as being twice married to Elizabeth Taylor, was also a Shakespearian actor viewed at one point as being the natural heir to Olivier. While Reed and Harris didn't quite capture as many awards, they did capture many hearts, with Harris continuing to enjoy popularity later in his life for his roles in major international films.

To celebrate this notorious foursome, arguably some of the most talented actors of their generation, we felt a Corpse Reviver was only appropriate. As the name suggests, this drink sits in the category of 'pick-me-up' cocktails, prescribed by bartenders to revive the souls that appeared in their bars feeling worse for wear. We have based our cocktail upon the Corpse Reviver No.4, to create our Corpse Reviver No.4.1.

HOLLYWOOD HELLRAISERS: CORPSE REVIVER Nº.4.1

Tequila

Mezcal

Lillet Blanc

Cointreau

Grapefruit and lime Oleo Saccharum

Absinthe

Grapefruit coin, to garnish

Citrusy, smoky and enlivening

One of the earliest recollections of the Corpse Reviver appears in an 1861 edition of the English weekly satirical magazine *Punch*. In the 1930 *Savoy Cocktail Book*, two recipes are given: Corpse Reviver No.1 was to be taken before 11am, and Corpse Reviver No.2 came with the warning that more than four will 'unrevive the corpse again'. No.3 was published in 1934 and No.4 was adapted in Sweden by Mans Dahlman, who had a preference for tequila.

The Corpse Reviver at Larry's is built to add even more body and life. With a touch of smokiness from the mezcal and extra aromatic notes from our homemade Oleo Saccharum, it makes for a refreshing long finish. Our Oleo Saccharum is made by peeling the skins off grapefruits and limes, and vacuum-sealing them with caster sugar and agave for 24 hours. This technique extracts all of the natural oils from the skins, which then mix with the sugar to create a beautiful citrusy syrup.

SONGS OF SOHO

ABOVE: Jimi Hendrix by Gered Mankowitz, 1967
NEXT SPREAD: Shirley Bassey by Angus McBean, 1959

Soho has long been the beating heart of London's music scene, from world-famous recording studios to the 'Tin Pan Alley' of Denmark Street, the haberdasheries, costumiers and media offices of Soho Square, to iconic music venues including the Marquee Club, the Shim Sham Club and the revered jazz club Ronnie Scott's.

Soho has launched the careers of some of the greatest musicians in the world. Elton John (then Reg Dwight) and David Bowie (then David Jones) would sit having a coffee together at La Gioconda café on Denmark Street waiting for odd jobs and their big break. In 1969 Elton John found in Gus Dudgeon a producer for Bowie's first hit 'Space Oddity' – perfectly timed for the lunar landing. It is thought that Bowie's left-handed guitar style in his Ziggy Stardust performances was a tribute to Jimi Hendrix, and it was at Ronnie Scott's that Hendrix played his stunning final performance. The many inimitable artists that have graced Ronnie's stage include Ella Fitzgerald, Amy Winehouse, George Melly and Johnny Griffin, as well as Shirley Bassey.

Nearby was Trident Studio where Bowie's 'Space Oddity' and 'Ziggy Stardust', and The Beatles' 'Hey Jude' were recorded. And close to that was the 2i's Coffee Bar on Wardour Street, famous for being the birthplace of British rock 'n' roll, with both Tommy Steele and Cliff Richard having been discovered there.

The name of the album *Songs of Pigalle* – Shirley Bassey's first live album, recorded in 1965 on the opening night of an eight-week residency at the Pigalle nightclub near Piccadilly – has inspired the name of our drink. Here we pay homage to the legendary and distinctive voices of the singers who have performed and spent time in London's Soho.

SONGS OF SOHO: ROSÉ MANHATTAN

Fettercairn Scotch whisky

Cadello 88

Dry vermouth

Mirabeau Rosé

Akashi-Tai Shiraume umeshu

Dr. Hostetter's bitter

Served over a large, roughly hewn ice cube

Dry ice and maraschino cherry, to garnish

Subtle, refined and aromatic

The Rosé Manhattan harks back to the Manhattan cocktail, which has a rich history dating back to the late 19th century. Its origins are believed to be tied to the Manhattan Club in New York City, where it was crafted for a banquet hosted by Winston Churchill's mother in the 1870s. The cocktail has become a staple in the world of mixology for its timeless appeal and versatility.

Our Manhattan-based cocktail was developed closely with Charles Moriarty, whose 2003 image of Amy Winehouse – taken on a trip to Manhattan for the cover of her debut album *Frank* – is in the National Portrait Gallery's Collection. The cocktail combines strength of character with the fleeting beauty of a song heard in a moment but lasting forever in memory, represented by its smoky presentation.

OPPOSITE: Songs of Soho

DIAMONDS
IN SOHO

ABOVE: Francis Bacon and Lucian Freud (detail) by Harry Diamond, 1974
NEXT SPREAD: Johnny Griffin by Harry Diamond, 1974

The West End has long been a melting pot of culture and creativity. At its heart is Soho, an ever-changing network of interwoven streets, filled with cafes, bars and clubs.

Photographers such as Ida Kar, Daniel Farson, Peter Stark and Harry Diamond captured London life in the post-war period. This cocktail was created in honour of Harry Diamond, an unsung hero of 20th century British photography. Diamond started his career as a stagehand before discovering the 35mm camera. He often drank in Soho, and became known as the man in the mac who was always carrying his camera in his pocket, capturing the artistic and cultural movements of the 1960s onwards.

Diamond is famous for having photographed a range of artists including Francis Bacon, Lucian Freud and Frank Auerbach, as well as Michael Clark, who helped us develop three cocktails for this book. Diamond is also noted for his photography of the pioneering jazz musicians of the 1960s and 70s, particularly around Soho, including Johnny Griffin, Snub Mosley, Viola Wills and Ronnie Scott.

Diamond really did capture many of the diamonds in Soho, and in this cocktail we try to capture the many influences of this famous entertainment district.

DIAMONDS IN SOHO: CHAMPAGNE PORNSTAR MARTINI

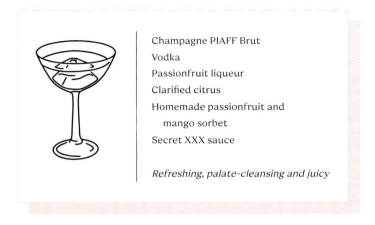

Champagne PIAFF Brut

Vodka

Passionfruit liqueur

Clarified citrus

Homemade passionfruit and
    mango sorbet

Secret XXX sauce

Refreshing, palate-cleansing and juicy

This is a twist on two different cocktails – the Sgroppino and the Pornstar Martini – that both reflect the melting pot of Soho.

The Sgroppino is an Italian cocktail, smooth and easy to finish – a sparkling drink-dessert hybrid that would have been served in many of the Italian restaurants that have historically populated Soho. Originally invented in Venice, it was intended as a palate-cleanser between courses.

The passionfruit in our sorbet alludes to the much-loved Pornstar Martini cocktail, a subtle nod to Soho nightlife, and our champagne top-up is a reference to Francis Bacon and his love of bubbly.

COLONY ROOM
GREEN

ABOVE: Muriel Belcher by John Deakin, c.1964
NEXT SPREAD: Kate Moss and Damien Hirst (detail) by Johnnie Shand Kydd, 1997

Soho's history is full of legendary landlords and landladies. However, perhaps no landlord or landlady has a legacy to match Muriel Belcher, who founded the private members' drinking club, the Colony Room, at 41 Dean Street, in 1948.

The club, often known simply as 'Muriel's', with its green and mirrored interior, played host to a wide range of London's bohemian characters. From artists, writers, musicians and thespians, to landed gentry, to Soho's barrow boys; Muriel's welcomed them all, as long as they spent well and were 'not bores'.

The club's most famous member was Francis Bacon, who said, 'I find the worse the hangover the more the mind seems to crackle with energy.' The Colony Room was both an inspiration and a sanctuary for him, and its influence can be seen in works such as his 1959 painting – with a distinctive green background – entitled *Miss Muriel Belcher*.

After Belcher's death, the club passed to her loyal (if sometimes abrasive) barman Ian Board, and became a cultural magnet for the Young British Artists (YBAs), including Damien Hirst, Sarah Lucas and Tracey Emin. By the turn of the century, the club's third proprietor, Michael Wojas, persuaded famous members, including Kate Moss and Daniel Craig, to serve drinks behind the bar.

The spirit of innovation and creativity fostered by Belcher and her club resonates with the adventurous spirit of mixology, inspiring bartenders to continually push boundaries and create new cocktail experiences. It is in their honour that we present a Mojito unlike any other.

COLONY ROOM GREEN: MOJITO

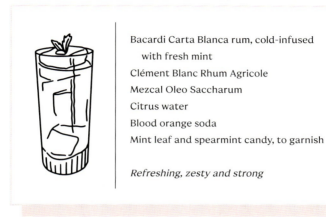

Bacardi Carta Blanca rum, cold-infused
   with fresh mint
Clément Blanc Rhum Agricole
Mezcal Oleo Saccharum
Citrus water
Blood orange soda
Mint leaf and spearmint candy, to garnish

Refreshing, zesty and strong

To celebrate the Colony Room, we enlisted the kind help of artist Michael Clark, who was one of the many artists whom Muriel Belcher took under her wing. Clark started his London life working behind the bar of the Colony Room. This is the first in a trilogy of colour-based cocktails developed with Clark.

Belcher was not a lover of cocktails – they were not sold at the Colony Room – but her one true love was people. In her honour we have selected the ever-popular Mojito, which shot onto the international scene in 1950s, aided by the hard-drinking Ernest Hemingway.

The drink is coloured the distinctive green shade of the Colony Room. It was critical to us that the colour was naturally derived, as Belcher prized honesty above everything else. The drink comes with a small, refreshing spearmint candy, to be eaten after the first sip.

FRANCIS BACON
ORANGE

Francis Bacon was born in 1909, in Dublin, Ireland. Despite a troubled childhood and being untrained in the arts, he grew to become one of the most influential and unique figurative artists of the 20th century, having found life-changing inspiration at a Picasso show in Paris.

In the 1930s, Bacon settled in London, drawn to the bohemian openness of the West End and its bars, restaurants and casinos. He struck up an immediate rapport with Muriel Belcher, the founder of the Colony Room, who grew to be a mother figure for him in place of his somewhat estranged family. Belcher gave him a weekly allowance of £10 to entertain friends there and the club would go on to become synonymous with him and the greatest British artists of his generation.

Cecil Beaton became friendly with Bacon after being introduced to him by the painter Graham Sutherland, and often drank with his group of artist friends around Soho. Beaton photographed Bacon several times from the early 1950s onwards, with the image opposite being an early example, showing the youthful Bacon against the backdrop of the richly decorated dressing room at Beaton's home.

To create our cocktail in celebration of Bacon, we worked closely with artist Michael Clark, who knew Bacon from the Colony Room and whose graphite portrait of him resides in the British Museum. Clark was inspired by the colour orange, which was Bacon's favourite colour. The short but powerful negroni forms the base of the cocktail and an effervescent and showy Champagne foam 'head' represents Bacon's personal sense of exuberance. Champagne was Bacon's favourite drink and he is reputed to have declared, 'Champagne for my friends, real pain for my sham friends'.

FRANCIS BACON ORANGE: CHAMPAGNE NEGRONI

Engine gin

Disaronno

El Bandarra Al Fresco

Pama Pomegranate liqueur

Citrus water

Grapefruit bitters

Crowned with our Champagne foam

Finely grated orange zest, to garnish

Textural, complex and indulgent

The Negroni is a timeless classic, known for its perfect balance of bitter, sweet, and herbal flavours. With a history dating back to early 20th century Italy, it is attributed to Count Camillo Negroni, who supposedly requested to strengthen his Americano cocktail by replacing the soda water with gin at the Caffè Casoni in Florence, around 1919.

This variation pays homage to the classic cocktail while adding modern flair and complexity. Engine gin brings botanical depth and character, while Disaronno adds a hint of nutty sweetness. The luxurious Champagne foam pays homage to Francis Bacon and adds the spirit of celebration and indulgence.

JARMAN BLUE

ABOVE: Derek Jarman by Steve Pyke, 1983
NEXT SPREAD: Derek Jarman by Trevor Leighton, 1990

Derek Jarman, like Francis Bacon, made an indelible imprint on British society. Jarman was a visionary filmmaker, artist and gay rights activist. His multifaceted career spanned various forms of creative expression, from experimental film to gardening, each marked by a distinctive, avant-garde approach.

Jarman's collaboration with musicians, including directing music videos for bands like The Smiths and Pet Shop Boys, fused his filmmaking with the musical styles of the 1970s and 1980s. Through the 1980s, he lived above the Phoenix Theatre on Charing Cross Road and could often be found in Soho or at the Blitz club.

Jarman's filmmaking was characterised by a unique aesthetic that combined vivid imagery with poignant themes. One of his notable connections in the film industry was with Laurence Olivier, who came out of retirement to appear in the poetic 1989 film *War Requiem*, in what was to be his last screen performance.

This cocktail, our third developed with Michael Clark, is inspired by one of Jarman's most profound works: his 1993 film *Blue*. It consisted of a single shot of the colour blue and a soundtrack where actors, including Jarman himself, narrated experiences of living with AIDS. *Blue* served as a powerful and deeply personal meditation on life.

In the later years of his life, Jarman retired to Prospect Cottage in Dungeness, Kent. Here he found solace in creating a garden that reflected his artistic sensibilities. Cultivated in the harsh, windswept coastal landscape, Jarman's garden became a symbol of resilience. It stands as a testament to his creativity and his ability to find beauty in the most unlikely places, and we have taken inspiration from this to create a unique cocktail.

JARMAN BLUE: AVIATION

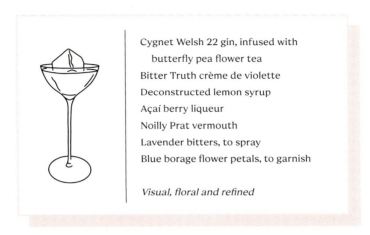

Cygnet Welsh 22 gin, infused with
    butterfly pea flower tea
Bitter Truth crème de violette
Deconstructed lemon syrup
Açaí berry liqueur
Noilly Prat vermouth
Lavender bitters, to spray
Blue borage flower petals, to garnish

Visual, floral and refined

The Aviation cocktail was created by Hugo Ensslin while working at the Hotel Wallick in New York City in 1916, inspired by the early era of aeronautics. Crème de violette gives it a distinctive blue colour.

We have taken inspiration from Jarman's beloved garden at Prospect Cottage, where lavender and wild flowers flourish in the salt air.

The cocktail is served in an elegant glass, with a translucent, roughly hewn ice cube, to give a feeling of beauty and strength yet fragility, making this one of our most delicate and surprising drinks.

OPPOSITE: Jarman Blue

MEET, SHOOT AND LEAVE!

ABOVE: Trojan and Leigh Bowery by David Gwinnutt, 1983
NEXT SPREAD: David Bowie by Terry O'Neill, 1974

Photographer David Gwinnutt captured the excitement of the underground queer art scene of the 1980s that transformed film, fashion and art. Coming out of the punk movement, he rebelled against the idea of the 'perfect' print and technical excellence. In contrast to the earlier work of photographers such as Cecil Beaton and Angus McBean, Gwinnutt's images are grainy and immediate. His portrait encounters were notoriously quick, prompting one sitter to comment that 'He meets, shoots and leaves!'

Gwinnutt's work captures the (now) famous creatives of experimental and anti-mainstream club nights such as Blitz, where according to legend, David Bowie was allowed in but Mick Jagger once wasn't. The door was run by Steve Strange and Rusty Egan, who went on to form the band Visage and were among the most influential people around the New Romantic movement of the early 1980s. Some of the 'Blitz kids', a group of young creatives and students, went on to star as extras in Bowie's 'Ashes to Ashes' video – for a time the most expensive pop video ever made.

Among many others, Gwinnutt photographed Leigh Bowery, an iconic Australian figure living in London, who expressed himself through elaborate fetishistic costumes and influenced many contemporary fashion designers. The creatively fertile period documented by Gwinnutt arguably laid the groundwork for the cultural global explosion of British-based music, fashion and art that we continue to enjoy today.

When we asked Gwinnutt to select his preferred cocktail, he chose the Espresso Martini, invented by former Colony Room barman and master mixologist, Dick Bradsell.

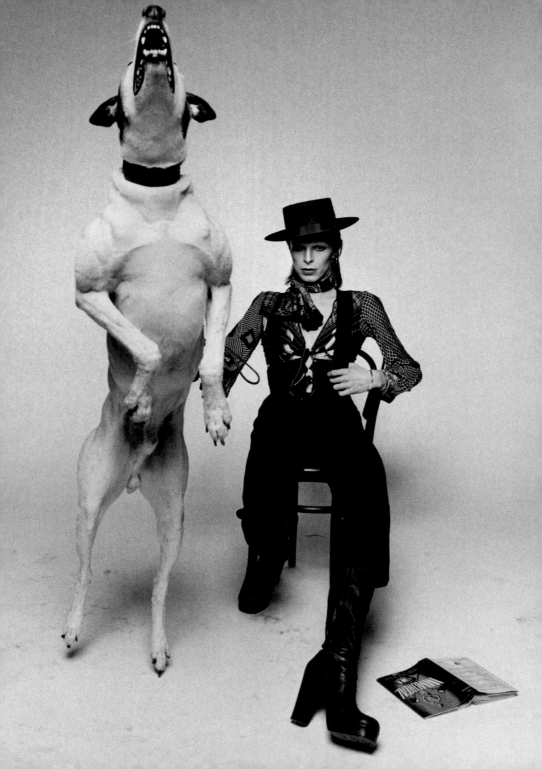

MEET, SH∞T AND LEAVE: ESPRESSO MARTINI

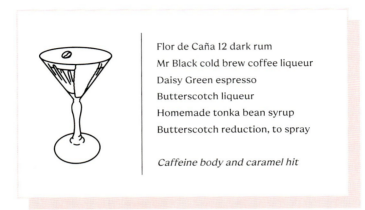

Flor de Caña 12 dark rum
Mr Black cold brew coffee liqueur
Daisy Green espresso
Butterscotch liqueur
Homemade tonka bean syrup
Butterscotch reduction, to spray

Caffeine body and caramel hit

The genius behind this deliciously smooth cocktail invention was British bartending guru Dick Bradsell. The story goes that Bradsell created the drink – originally called The Vodka Espresso – at Fred's Club in the late 1980s, when a famous model sidled up to the bar and asked for something to 'wake me up and f**k me up'. Bradsell's solution was a combination of vodka, fresh espresso, coffee liqueur and sugar, shaken into a moreishly bittersweet mix. The Espresso Martini is now a worldwide classic.

Our version was developed with David Gwinnutt and has smoother tasting notes; a dark rum base and butterscotch liqueur with hints of coffee, chocolate, and caramel. Our homemade syrup involves toasting our Daisy Green coffee with tonka beans for a few minutes, before adding filtered water, dark soft brown sugar and vanilla.

AUSSIES BY THE BAR

ABOVE: Peter Finch by Michael Ward, 1960

NEXT SPREAD: Leigh Bowery by David Gwinnutt, c.1983

As Daisy Green is an Australian-inspired business, we felt obliged to prop a few of our fellow Antipodeans by the bar.

On the wall at Larry's is a portrait of Peter Finch, the British-Australian actor who became one of cinema's most celebrated stars. It was Laurence Olivier who encouraged Finch to return to London after many years in Australia. Finch became a star of the West End stage, as well as acting in films in the UK and Hollywood. He could regularly be found in Soho, drinking with the 'hellraisers', but also described himself as a Buddhist, and was a writer of poetry. Finch and co-star Faye Dunaway won Academy Awards for their roles in the film *Network* (1976), for Best Actor and Best Actress respectively. Dunaway can be seen with her Oscar in Terry O'Neill's iconic portrait, on the cover of this book. O'Neill was married to Dunaway for a short time and many of his images of stars of fashion, cinema and music, as well as the British royal family, can be seen at the National Portrait Gallery.

69

Alongside Finch, we toast Australian icon Leigh Bowery. As creator of the London club night Taboo, Bowery played an important role in club culture and worked as a costume designer and performer. In the 1990s, Bowery created controversial performances with his band Minty, and modelled for Lucian Freud.

In their honour, we present both our classic Raspberry Sour and an alcohol-free version of it. A firm favourite, it's hard to go wrong with this gorgeous pink cocktail. With or without alcohol, this one is perfect for the morning after.

AUSSIES BY THE BAR: RASPBERRY SOUR

Bombay Sapphire gin
Fresh lemon juice
Homemade raspberry syrup
Foam bitters
Freeze-dried raspberries, to garnish

Rejuvenating, fruity and pretty in pink!

Here we pay homage to Daisy Green's Australian roots with one of our most iconic cocktails – the Raspberry Sour. Vibrant and striking, it celebrates the Australian icons in the National Portrait Gallery's Collection.

Raspberries grow in abundance in Australia and are often a feature of classic Australian dishes the pavlova and the lamington. Our raspberry syrup is homemade, using fresh raspberries cooked in a pan with filtered water and caster sugar: we let it boil and then cool before filtering, ready to use.

This cocktail can be converted to being non-alcoholic by replacing the gin with a dry non-alcoholic 'gin' such as Strykk or Lyre's. Adding tonic water or soda water creates a delightful non-alcoholic spritz, which is best served in a highball glass.

THE MACCARITA

ABOVE: Paul McCartney by Clive Arrowsmith, 1976
NEXT SPREAD: Paul McCartney by Linda McCartney, 1968
FINAL SPREAD: George Harrison by Paul McCartney, 1964

We are delighted to end the book with the Maccarita, our version of Sir Paul McCartney's take on the Margarita.

On its 2023 reopening, the National Portrait Gallery hosted a new exhibition, *Paul McCartney Photographs 1963–64: Eyes of the Storm*, sharing for the first time McCartney's photographs taken with a 35mm camera as Beatlemania erupted in the UK and across the world. Few of these photographs had previously been seen beyond McCartney's immediate family and friends, having been stored for almost sixty years in his personal archive. The uniquely personal images documented an intense period as The Beatles travelled from Liverpool to London, then to Paris, New York, Washington D.C. and finally, to technicolour Miami. It was during this time that the band rose from national sensation to international phenomenon.

The exhibition was named *Eyes of the Storm* as opposed to 'the eye of the storm' to better reflect the many faces and perspectives of the moment. This captures the essence of portraiture, which is as much about the viewer as it is about the subject, time and society.

This cocktail is born out of music, love and family. We seek to serve it to you as if McCartney had made it himself, and we can't thank him enough for allowing us to include it here.

Enjoy.

Oh – one rule. No more than two!

THE MACCARITA: MARGARITA

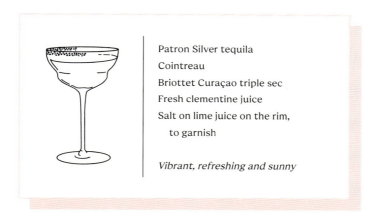

Patron Silver tequila
Cointreau
Briottet Curaçao triple sec
Fresh clementine juice
Salt on lime juice on the rim,
    to garnish

Vibrant, refreshing and sunny

The Maccarita pays homage to the Margarita, with its history as colourful as its flavours, and various stories claiming to be its true origin. Tequila, which gained popularity in the United States after the Second World War, is the key ingredient in a good margarita. The spirit is made only in the Mexican town of Tequila, from blue Weber agave.

During the 1970s, a Tequila Sunrise was the drink in LA, loved by many of the greatest music icons. With its key ingredients of orange and tequila, it has some similarities with the Maccarita. McCartney likes to use clementine juice in his cocktail, and includes triple sec and Cointreau to add layers of orange which contrast with the lime, salt and tequila blanco. At Larry's, we have played with a number of twists on this drink – the peppery tequila blanco can be switched for tequila resposado with a hint of vanilla, or for a smoky mezcal.

NOTES AND CREDITS

A Note from the Author:

For those interested in making the classic versions of the cocktails in this book, information can be found at Diffords, who have guides on their website and produce stunning cocktail books authored by Simon Difford, including *365 Days of Cocktails* (Octopus, 2015). Otherwise, we are fans of Harry Craddock's original *Savoy Cocktail Book* (Chump Change, 1930 / Little, Brown, 2014), Dick Bradsell's book *Dicktales* (Mixellany, 2022) and Harry MacElhone's *ABC of Mixing Cocktails* (Dean and Son, 1930 / Martino Fine Books, 2017). All were immensely helpful sources of information when writing this book and looking for inspiration for Larry's cocktails.

Picture Credits:

The National Portrait Gallery would like to thank the copyright holders for granting permission to reproduce works illustrated in this book. Every effort has been made to contact the holders of copyright material, and any omissions will be corrected in future editions if the publisher is notified in writing.

All works are © National Portrait Gallery, London, unless otherwise noted.

p.2 Betty Cowell, by Yevonde, 1935, x222563, purchased with support from the Portrait Fund, 2021. p.4 Vivien Leigh, Kay Kendall, Noël Coward and Lauren Bacall, by Keystone Press Agency Ltd, 1959, x139808, given by Terence Pepper, 2014. p.8 *Cara Delevingne (The Red Lion #1)*, by Miles Aldridge, 2012, x200100 © Miles Aldridge, 2012. p.10 Laurence Olivier, photograph by Yousuf Karsh, 1954, P490(59), given by Yousuf Karsh, 1991 © Yousuf Karsh, Camera Press London. p.12 x36099, acquired from Daily Herald, 1980. p.14 x223231, purchased with

support from the Portrait Fund, 2021. p.16 x220439, purchased with support from the Portrait Fund, 2021. p.18 x40432, accepted in lieu of tax by H.M. Government and allocated to the Gallery, 1991 © Cecil Beaton Archive, Condé Nast. p.20 P1489, given by Mr Ford Hill and the American Friends of the National Portrait Gallery (London) © Cecil Beaton / Victoria and Albert Museum, London. p.22 x40277, accepted in lieu of tax by H.M. Government and allocated to the Gallery, 1991 © Cecil Beaton Archive, Condé Nast. p.24 x40266, accepted in lieu of tax by H.M. Government and allocated to the Gallery, 1991 © Cecil Beaton Archive, Condé Nast. p.28 P937 © Estate of Angus McBean / National Portrait Gallery, London. p.30 x131152, given by EMI, 2007 © Harvard Theatre Collection, Houghton Library, Harvard University. p.32 x87244. p.34 x132853, given by Adrian Woodhouse, 2006. Courtesy Adrian Woodhouse. p.36 x8344 © Bob Willoughby / mptvimages. com. p.38 P910 © Houghton Library, Harvard University. p.40 x126233 © Gered Mankowitz / Iconic Images. p.42 P885 © Harvard Theatre Collection, Houghton Library, Harvard University. p.46 x135768, bequeathed by Harry Diamond, 2012. p.48 x210168, bequeathed by Harry Diamond, 2012. p.50 © John Deakin / John Deakin Archive / Bridgeman Images. p.52 x87679 © Johnnie Shand Kydd. p.54 x40008, accepted in lieu of tax by H.M. Government and allocated to the Gallery, 1991 © Cecil Beaton Archive, Condé Nast. p.56 P587 © 1963 Condé Nast Publications Inc. p.58 x27429 © Steve Pyke. p.60 x35318, given by Trevor Leighton, 1990 © Trevor Leighton / National Portrait Gallery, London. p.64 x131399 © David Gwinnutt / National Portrait Gallery, London. p.66 x126130, given by Terry O'Neill, 2003 © Iconic Images / Terry O'Neill. p.68 x46673 © Michael Ward Archives / National Portrait Gallery, London. p.70 x199663 © David Gwinnutt / National Portrait Gallery, London. p.72 Paul McCartney, photograph by Clive Arrowsmith, 1976, x199700, given by Clive Arrowsmith, 2016 © Clive Arrowsmith, Camera Press London. p.74 x128729, given by the estate of Linda McCartney, 2006 © Paul McCartney. p.76 © 1963–64 Paul McCartney under exclusive license to MPL Archive LLP.

pp.26, 44, 62 and endpapers: painting by Tabby Riley and Sarah Crane.
pp.6, 26, 27, 44, 45, 62, 63 and endpapers: photographs courtesy of Daisy Green Collection © Melisa Coppola.
pp.13, 17, 21, 25, 31, 35, 39, 43, 49, 53, 57, 61, 67, 71, 75: cocktail drawings courtesy of Daisy Green Collection © Jennifer Tims.

ACKNOWLEDGEMENTS

Our first thanks are to the amazing icons who adorn the walls at Larry's and feature in this book. These incredible images – and the memories, anecdotes, inspiration and excitement that accompany them – are what bring us all together.

Creating these drinks would be impossible to do without our cocktail team, Tomasz Marcisz, Vito Verrengia and Salvatore Distefano, whose passion, commitment and skills are unrivalled.

A raft of hugely talented artists have graciously allowed us to include their work in this book. Particular thanks must also go to David Gwinnutt, Charles Moriarity and Michael Clark for the time, effort and enthusiasm they have given in helping us develop our Meet, Shoot and Leave!, Songs of Soho, Colony Room Green, Francis Bacon Orange and Jarman Blue cocktails.

Thank you to the National Portrait Gallery Trustees, Directorate and Curatorial teams, without whom Larry's would not have been possible. To David Ross, Nicholas Cullinan, Anna Starling, Clare Freestone, Sabina Jaskot-Gill and the wider team, we cannot thank you enough.

Working on this book alongside the National Portrait Gallery's publishing and rights teams – Kara Green, Laura Cherry, Priti Kothary, Jemma Jacobs, Taylor C. Bentley, Zoe Bott, Mark Lynch, Myriam Upton and Katie Anderson, with designer, Charlotte Heal – has been great fun, and we are indebted to you all.

We are immensely grateful to Sir Paul McCartney and his team for their generosity of spirit and support in allowing us to serve the Maccarita and feature it in this book.

Thank you to Darren Coffield, who kindly provided insight and help with the historical elements of the book. The world of drinking is one of myth and legend, and though we have endeavoured to be as accurate as possible here, we apologise if any of the storytelling has been misremembered.

We are grateful to Daisy Green's artists, who have been with us on our journey since 2012 and have always supported our passion for creativity. Huge thanks to Jennifer Tims for illustrations and Melisa Coppola for photography featured here. Thank you to Justin Hibbs and Alan McFeltridge who mastered, printed and framed all 100+ pieces at Larry's; and to Tabby Riley and Sarah Crane for their work on the beautiful pink walls at Larry's that are featured throughout this book.

Finally ... thank you to our customers. Without your support, creating these spaces and this book would not be possible.

Tom Onions and Prue Freeman
Founders: The Daisy Green Collection

Published in Great Britain by National Portrait Gallery Publications

National Portrait Gallery

St Martin's Place

London WC2H 0HE

Every purchase supports the National Portrait Gallery, London. For a complete catalogue
of current publications, please visit our website at www.npg.org.uk/publications

Text by Tom Onions

ISBN 978 1 85514 539 9

A catalogue record for this book is available from the British Library

10 9 8 7 6 5 4 3 2

Director of Commercial and Operations: Anna Starling

Senior Publishing Manager: Kara Green

Project Editor: Laura Cherry

Picture Research: Katie Anderson

Production Manager: Priti Kothary

Proofreader: Taylor C. Bentley

Publishing Assistant: Jemma Jacobs

Design: Charlotte Heal Design

Printed and bound in Italy by Printer Trento

Reproduction by DL Imaging

Front cover image: Faye Dunaway by Terry O'Neill, 1977, National Portrait Gallery, London, x126147.
Given by Terry O'Neill, 2003 © Iconic Images / Terry O'Neill

Always remember to drink responsibly. Women who are pregnant or trying to conceive should avoid
alcohol. In the UK, the NHS recommends that men and women should drink no more than 14 units
of alcohol per week, with one unit equal to about a single small (25ml) measure of spirits. In the US,
the Department of Health and Human Services defines moderate drinking as no more than one drink per
day for women and no more than two drinks per day for men.

DAISY I GREEN